~

MILLIONAIRES' HANDBOOK

BY H. PETER R. MILLER

Words of Worth...
Sage advice for success in business and life

~

World Leisure Corporation
Boston

Distributed to the trade in the U.S.A. by
Midpoint Trade Books, Inc.,
27 W. 20th Street, Suite 1102, New York, NY 10011,
Tel. (212) 727-0190, fax (212) 727-0195.

Distributed to the trade in U.K. by
Portfolio, Unit 1c, West Ealing Business Centre,
Alexandria Road, London W13 0NJ United Kingdom.
Tel. (0181) 579-7748, fax (0181) 567-0904.

Distributed to the trade in Canada by
Hushion House, 36 Northline Road,
Toronto, Ontario, M4B 3E2, Canada
Tel. (416) 287-3146, fax (416) 287-0081
Internet: www.hushion.com.

Mail Order, Catalog, other International sales and rights,
and Special Sales by
World Leisure, PO Box 160, Hampstead, NH 03841.
Tel. (877) 863-1966, fax (603) 947-0838
E-mail: wleisure@aol.com; Internet: www.worldrec.com.

ISBN: 0-915009-70-6

~

MILLIONAIRES' HANDBOOK

~

Contents

Millionaires' approach to life 9

Passion for life 75

Education 82

Frugality 84

Negotiations 98

Proverbs 113

Family 126

Employees 133

Isn't it the truth 154

Persistence 184

Biographies 187

Introduction

Welcome to the world of millionaires.

For years I have been fascinated with the world's richest people. I wanted to know how they did it — how they succeeded. I wondered if there were any secrets or insights that might help me on my way to my first million.

I studied what millionaires said. Here are many of the quotes and stories I found most valuable

I asked what they considered important. Here are their answers.

I learned that success does not come easily. These millionaires learned many lessons as they made their way to the top. Here they are sharing the basic truths that have paved their way to wealth and happiness.

One of the most important lessons learned while researching this book is that money was rarely the main goal in their life.

They each worked to succeed at something they loved and believed in, or to find a way to take control of their own time, so that they could pursue other personal dreams of public service, family, creativity or travel.

In these pages, you will find a veritable business school degree of sayings and truths that have served some of the world's most successful people well on their road to riches.

These sayings, lessons and aphorisms have been collected both from the famous as well as from the often-unknown millionaire next door. In many cases these millionaires want to remain anonymous; in others we reveal their identities.

You will learn from many who have made a name for themselves in businesses as different as the Internet and grocery stores.

For instance, Steve Jenkins was a founder of two Internet startups long before the Internet was cool. Darryl Jorgensen started an elevator company in Los Angeles. John Knab is CEO of Fonex Broadband Corporation. Dan Roberts is a financial consultant. Klaus Lassig worked for the same company for 25 years from dawn 'til near midnight and now owns his own business.

Mel Marion produced and starred in a children's TV show, taught school, ran a riding school, and sold real estate.

S. Lee Ross, a CPA for 20 years, made his fortune by investing in oil fields and gas production.

John Walton is the CEO of Doors Plus
Inc., making luxurious doors for million-
dollar homes.

Whether you are on your way to your
first million dollars or contuning to add
to your fortune, I hope these invaluable
insights and lessons help smooth the
path in both your business life and
personal relationships.

H. Peter R. Miller

Millionaires' approach to life

*"People who can step back and look
at the big picture will make it,
while the bean counters rarely do."*
John Walton

*"Think people, expect quality,
and plan for results."*
John Simcox

"Be organized.
Most of the missed opportunities
lay in the pile of papers on your desk."
Steve Jenkins

"The American system of ours gives
each and every one of us a great
opportunity if we only seize it with
both hands and make the most of it."
Al Capone — net worth 1.3 million

*"If people don't think you
have money, then no one
will ask you for it."*
Millionaire — net worth 2.7 million

"Say what everyone else is thinking."
Millionaire — net worth 4.5 million

*"If you don't have the ability
to control the events in your life,
life will control you."*
Charles Hobbs

"When everyone is wrong,
everyone is right."
— La Chaussee

"I don't care how much
money you make,
you can't buy back your integrity."
Steve Jenkins

"If you want to test a stock broker,
ask to see his personal portfolio."
Millionaire — net worth 10 million

"Much of life is sales:
lawyers sell the jury,
politicians sell themselves,
writers sell ideas.
If you can sell
you'll always have a job."
Millionaire — net worth 4 million

"Always be prepared to lose everything
and be happy."
Millionaire — net worth 95 million

"Completely new ideas are riskier than improving existing products, but they can be a great deal more profitable."
Millionaire — net worth 5.5 million

"Integrity is not a renewable asset."
Millionaire — net worth 1.8 million

"When you give a lot, you learn a lot. I learned a great deal from CEOs at community service projects."
Max Farash

*"Keep a record of every conversation,
experience, everything you gain."*
Paul Allen

*"Remember to focus on increasing the
value of your company not the profits."*
Millionaire — net worth 5 million

*"Time is not money,
it's more valuable."*
Steve Jenkins

*"As a salesman, I found
I was rejected on average about
seven times before I made a sale."*
Millionaire — net worth 6 million

*"The ability to focus on and
accomplish the most vital priorities
equals concentration of power."*
Charles Hobbs

*"Don't be late
because you tried to do too much."*
Millionaire — net worth 5.4 million

*"It's easy to be unfair in business.
I had opportunities to bully, but years
later my relationships paid off when
starting a new venture and the banks
didn't want to know me."*
Dave Perry

*"It doesn't take a brain surgeon to buy
bananas at 50 cents a pound
and sell them for a dollar a pound.
In business you just have to be able to
execute and if you do that
day after day, you will succeed.
Most success is not glamorous."*
William D. Price

*"Avoid thinking,
'It's not my problem.'"*
Millionaire — net worth 2.7 million

"Mistakes can be made with clients as long as you follow through and follow up consistently and often."
Dan Roberts

"In sales and in life, ask questions where people have to respond in a way that automatically invites more info, like, 'Have you ever heard of product X?'"
Hal Wing

"I remember growing up without heat
huddled up to a potbelly stove
clutching the edges and thinking
'You're not going to live like this,
you're gonna be a millionaire.' "
Bill Raymond

"Ship on time, ship complete,
and delight the customer."
Kelly Dame

"Take responsibility—
Eve tempted Adam with the apple,
but God didn't blame the apple."
Dan Millstone

"A deal comes along every day.
Be selective when saying yes,
don't look back,
and be patient waiting for results."
Paul Hulme

*"Give your card out
as much as you can."*
Millionaire — net worth 4.1 million

"Speak two languages."
Millionaire — net worth 1.5 million

*"Make a flash card for every person
you know and how you know them."*
Millionaire — net worth 16 million

"I went into business to make a big splash, not to be just a drop in the pond—that's the only way to do it."
Darryl Jorgensen

"If you know the horse is going to win, you bet on it— I never had a plan B."
Darryl Jorgensen

"If you can do it yourself, you're better off without a partner."
Klaus K. Lassig

"Keep all of your promises no matter what. If I say I'll so something, I'll work 24 hours a day until it's done."
Klaus K. Lassig

"Lethargy bordering on sloth remains the cornerstone of our investment style."
Warren Buffett
— net worth 12 billion

"Trade services with other companies; it's two-way wholesale."
Millionaire — net worth 6.7 million

"Return every phone call; don't burn bridges because of laziness."
Millionaire — net worth 3.3 million

"True character is revealed under pressure and in the face of failure."
Millionaire — net worth 87 million

*"Never respond to a critic
unless he is right."*
Millionaire — net worth 2.3 million

*"You know better than anyone else
what you are capable of."*
Millionaire — net worth 6 million

*"I can't take risks
with other people's money."*
Max Farash

*"You will always be in business
if your product appeals to the
people who want to get rich."*
Millionaire — net worth 4.5 million

*"The best thing to do with your money
is put it back into your company."*
Millionaire — net worth 5 million

*"Know when details count
and make a list of them."*
Millionaire — net worth 3 million

"The 'soft sell' is the best
for anyone you want
a continued relationship with."
Millionaire — net worth 5 million

"Avoiding the appearance of wealth
makes you less of a target for crime
even though you could handle theft
better than those who appear rich."
Millionaire — net worth 6.5 million

*"To important people
you insist on explaining why,
to unimportant people
you insist on explaining how."*
Charles A. Coonradt

*"Resist the temptation
to divulge more information
because you are in a social setting."*
Millionaire — net worth 2.5 million

"Don't assume; clarify."
Millionaire — net worth 5.8 million

*"Don't ask your friend's opinion of a
product. Test the market."*
Millionaire — net worth 4.7 million

*"In social conversation,
always be more interested in
talking about the other person."*
Millionaire — net worth 3.6 million

*"Know what you do best and
hire someone to do that
which you do worst."*
Millionaire — net worth 5 million

*"Seek the reputation of
a man of action and judgement."*
Millionaire — net worth 47 million

*"Learn proper etiquette
in every aspect of life."*
Millionaire — net worth 4 million

"Growing up you must learn courage
—courage to sell yourself.
Run for student body office;
the point isn't winning it's trying."
Millionaire — net worth 21 million

"It's easier to make a thousand bucks
by selling 100 ten dollar items
than selling one product for a
thousand dollars."
Millionaire — net worth 5 million

*"If two tasks are equally important,
do the quick one first."*
Millionaire — net worth 2.3 million

*"Many times appearance becomes
reality, while reality fades away."*
Millionaire — net worth 2 million

*"A product or service should be so good
that people will decide to buy it
before seeing the price."*
Millionaire — net worth 3.9 million

*"Start businesses while you're young
when you've got nothing to lose."*
Millionaire — net worth 6.7 million

*"The way to a client's heart
is through his or her kids."*
Millionaire — net worth 4 million

*"Make daily, monthly
and long term goals."*
Millionaire — net worth 3.6 million

*"Components of success:
people skills, communication
and time management."*
John Simcox

*"Spend as much time selling others on
your decision as you spent making it."*
Millionaire — net worth 12 million

*"Thou shouldst not decide until thou
hast heard what both have to say."*
Aristophanes

"Doing your homework
is often better
than thinking fast on your feet."
Millionaire — net worth 4 million

"Don't be afraid to sell the customer
exactly what he needs.
He will keep coming back."
Millionaire — net worth 12 million

"Take old friends,

you never see,

out to lunch."

Millionaire — net worth 6 million

"Believe only half of what you see and

nothing that you hear."

— Dinah Mulock Craik

"Get a lawyer

and tell him everything."

Millionaire — net worth 6.5 million

*"If you plan on changing
as soon as you get rich,
it won't be a happy life."*
Millionaire — net worth 5 million

*"Don't hold clients to a contract if
things change. How would you feel if
the shoe were on the other foot?"*
Millionaire — net worth 3.1 million

*"I grow daily to honor facts more and
more, and theory less and less."*
Thomas Carlyle

"Be acutely aware of every opportunity. If you're sitting next to the CEO of the company you would love to work with, don't politely leave him alone just because he is a busy man."

Millionaire — net worth 3.1 million

"People like finishers better than starters."

Millionaire — net worth 3.3 million

"Bankers care about a trend for the next three years, not whether or not you are going to make a lot of money right off the bat."
John Simcox

"You can never underestimate luck — and while luck is important you have to be able to execute when an opportunity comes."
Michael Morgan

"*Staying late means
you just didn't finish;
coming early means
you want to do extra.*"
Millionaire — net worth 3.6 million

"*The best way to diffuse a scandal
is to confess the truth immediately.*"
Millionaire — net worth 35 million

"Employers make resumes seem important because they want an organized application process. If you can find another way to get a face to face interview, do it."
Millionaire — net worth 5.6 million

"If the sales pitch is long, it means the product needs a lot of building up to be appealing or the price is too high."
Millionaire — net worth 12 million

"If you want to go to work on the subway, sell to a person with a Rolls Royce. If you want to drive a Rolls Royce, sell to people on the subway."
Gene Friedman

"A good attorney will save you so much money—don't be afraid to pay for good advice."
Steve Jenkins

"A bad product or service will only sell once."
Millionaire — net worth 5.3 million

*"Use little opportunities of exposure
to make a good impression.
Think of ways you can stand out.
Remember people's names, their wives'
names, their kids' names."*
Millionaire — net worth 24 million

*"I don't ever re-invent the wheel,
I just try to make it faster."*
Dan Millstone

*"Find out what people are interested in
and talk about it."*
Millionaire — net worth 3.7 million

*"When you shoot for an eagle and
miss you hit a rock, but when you
shoot for the moon and miss
you may hit an eagle."*
Millionaire — net worth 5 million

*"Listen to people who know what they
are talking about—recognize that
they know their own business."*
Steve Jenkins

"Always be on your best behavior
with superiors no matter
how chummy it gets."
Millionaire — net worth 1.5 million

"Be careful of the goals you set, you
are almost sure to achieve them."
Millionaire — net worth 6.8 million

"Learn how to write good thank you
and proposal letters."
Millionaire — net worth 5 million

"One of the most powerful tools in a
good interview is realizing that
everyone you talk to,
until you have left the building,
is part of the interview."
Millionaire — net worth 5 million

"Learn to be as comfortable around the
presidents of companies as you are
around your own associates."
Millionaire — net worth 3 million

"The customer must be given
the best possible service.
Customers pay our salary.
We held annual round tables
where we brought them into our
facility to beat up our product
and give us feedback
on their needs.
They prioritized development."

Kyle Bowen Love

*"If you really want a job,
start by working for free."*
Millionaire — net worth 8 million

*"Doing more than you are expected
makes you the boss."*
Millionaire — net worth 2.5 million

*"Only use words everyone
understands, but use
impeccable grammar."*
Millionaire — net worth 6 million

"It takes the same amount of effort to
make your product look good as it does
to actually make it good."
Millionaire — net worth 6 million

"Ask yourself how other people,
who think differently,
would solve the same problem."
Millionaire — net worth 5 million

"A phone call is usually
better than a letter."
Millionaire — net worth 3.1 million

*"Common sense is in spite of,
not the result of, education."*
Victor Hugo

*"When you procrastinate
it often takes twice the time
to remember what it is you had to do."*
Millionaire — net worth 5 million

*"It's easier to gain fame after wealth,
but the best way is through excellence."*
Millionaire — net worth 100 million

"Being ethical is like farming—
for a long time it seems like a lot of
effort with no results."
Millionaire — net worth 4 million

"Work as if you're paying yourself
by the hour."
Millionaire — net worth 49 million

"Read articles outside
your usual interest."
Millionaire — net worth 5 million

*"Write longer letters to those who are
honored to hear from you and short
ones to everyone else."*
Millionaire — net worth 3.7 million

*"The best businesses are those
that provide valuable services
to people who have money."*
Millionaire — net worth 5 million

"Solve your boss' problems."
Millionaire — net worth 60 million

"Know when the best time to call people is. If you don't know, ask."

Millionaire — net worth 5.1 million

"Business is religion, and religion is business. The man who does not make a business of his religion has a religious life of no force, and the man who does not make a religion of his business has a business life of no character."

Maltbie Babcock

"Stick to your knitting.
The primary objective should always
be a good product no matter
how much you grow."
Millionaire — net worth 5 million

"For questions you can't or don't want
to answer, deflect them by rephrasing
them to the question you do want."
Millionaire — net worth 5.2 million

*"Write letters of admiration to
business men you look up to."*
Millionaire — net worth 5 million

*"If a client takes calls
during your meeting,
you're not important enough."*
Millionaire — net worth 6 million

*"You have to think like a businessman
and perform like an engineer."*
Kent Archibald

*"It saves time to meet with colleagues
in their offices. It's easier to leave than
to get them to leave."*
Millionaire — net worth 4.5 million

*"Almost all the millionaires I know,
made their own fortunes.
It's still a land of opportunity."*
Millionaire — net worth 6 million

"Gentlemen, you have undertaken to
cheat me. I will not sue you,
for the law takes too long.
I will ruin you."
Millionaire 1794-1877
— net worth 105 million

"Try to address every task
the first time you encounter it."
Millionaire — net worth 6 million

"Own the most inexpensive home in your neighborhood. Remember, in real estate it's location, location, location."

Millionaire — net worth 6 million

"We will either find a way or make one."

Hannibal

— net worth 500 million?

"All of business ethics in three words:
The Golden Rule."
Millionaire — net worth 5 million

"When aspiring to the highest place,
it is honorable to reach
the second or even the third rank."
Cicero

"If you look around, everything in this
world can be improved upon."
Hal Wing

*"Using the larger airlines
means more backup flights."*
Millionaire — net worth 5.8 million

*"Why will people spend thousands of
dollars for college but be afraid to
invest in a business?"*
**Millionaire (High School Dropout)
— net worth 12 million**

"Acting publicly forces good ethics."
Millionaire — net worth 35 million

"For a good accountant,
ask successful, reliable associates
whose trust will be on the line."
Millionaire — net worth 6.2 million

"No one has time
to do it right the second time."
Millionaire — net worth 3.3 million

"The best way to hang up on someone
is in the middle of your own sentence."
Millionaire — net worth 6 million

"When dining with a client,
always make reservations for three
to insure a comfortable table."
Millionaire — net worth 2.2 million

"The question, 'Who ought to be
boss?' is like asking, 'Who ought to be
the tenor in the quartet?' Obviously,
the man who can sing tenor."
Henry Ford — net worth 1.2 billion

"However inferior in wealth I may be to many who surround me, I would not exchange for their treasures the satisfaction I have of knowing I have done what has never before been accomplished by man . . . I would rather be at the head of a louse than at the tail of a lion."

Samuel Colt 1814-1862
(inventor of the Colt revolver)
— net worth 5 million

*"Buy a few shares of an
up-and-coming stock every year."*
Millionaire — net worth 5 million

*"Act like a duck, calm on the surface,
but paddle like a devil underneath."*
Millionaire — net worth 32 million

*"Don't keep putting money into a
business just because you are already
invested and you can't lose
what you've spent."*
Millionaire — net worth 47 million

"Spend time learning at the feet of
business tycoons."
Millionaire — net worth 3.7 million

"Try to think of one new need every
day and how to fill it."
Millionaire — net worth 5 million

"Your greatest opponent
can become your greatest ally
under different circumstances."
Millionaire — net worth 36 million

"We judge ourselves by what we feel
capable of doing, while others judge us
by what we have already done."
Henry Wadsworth Longfellow

"Half of your problems will be solved
if you can look through other
people's glasses."
Millionaire — net worth 2.3 million

"The problem with being a doctor or a lawyer is you have to spend your money to look successful. Would you hire an attorney who lives in the projects?"
Millionaire — net worth 5 million

"If you want to know the value of something, ask accounting and marketing and then average the two."
Millionaire — net worth 7 million

*"Entertain people
while providing substance."*
Millionaire — net worth 5 million

*"Executives need to be masters
of the rudimentary functions
of the business."*
Millionaire — net worth 5.3 million

*"Earn all you can. Save all you can.
Give all you can."*
Craig Earnshaw

*"Failure is in your head—
lots of things don't work
but they aren't failures."*
Leroy Spears

*"Never underestimate your
competitors. They are smart
and don't want you there."*
Millionaire — net worth 21 million

*"I skate to where the puck
is going to be."*
Wayne Grezsky

*"I look for people who are like
myself—a restless spirit
with an inquisitive mind."*
Max Farash

*"As an entrepreneur you must realize
that some banks will,
and some banks won't."*
John Simcox

*"Venture capitalists look at the
individual and then the concept —
you have to sell yourself."*
Gene Friedman

*"I think it is important for everyone
to have a good hard failure
when they're young."*
Walt Disney

*"Bite off more than you can chew,
and then chew it."*
Millionaire — net worth 4 million

"*Find the smartest guy in the field
and make him your partner.*"
Jonathan Coon

"*Listen to people who
know what they are talking about.
Your business is your business and
their business is their business.*"
Millionaire — net worth 7 million

*"Good neighbors need good fences.
Get good documentation so that you
can stay friends."*
Hal Wing

*"Focus on technology because old fart
competitors won't."*
Jonathan Coon

*"If you can visualize it you can do it.
Organize it in your mind
and if it's right,
all you have to do is execute."*
Bill Brady

Passion for life

*"Amassing a wealth of interesting
and varied experiences,
shared with people from many lands
and all walks of life,
is ultimately far more rewarding
than obtaining power or riches."*
Scott Parks Letellier

*"Follow your passion,
your passion will bleed excellence."*
Millionaire — net worth 4 million

*"I don't measure success
by how much money one has.
Success is self direction in acquiring
whatever one desires of life
which ultimately contributes
to everyone's peace, happiness
and personal satisfaction."*
Charles Hobbs

"Do what you love.
Know your own bone;
gnaw at it, bury it, unearth it,
and gnaw it still."
Thoreau

"Get as much education as you can
then follow your passion.
Your passion will breed excellence."
Norm Nemro

"Don't become an entrepreneur
because you hate your job.
Do it because you like your job
but you have a great idea and
would love to run your own business."
Millionaire — net worth 2.8 million

"Successful entrepreneurs work
within a large bubble
of passion and enthusiasm.
When that bubble pops
it is time to sell your company,
get out and move on."
Kyle Bowen Love

*"Making money so that you can spend
it should never be the focus."*
Millionaire — net worth 17 million

*"As a kid I didn't have anything to do
so I hung out at the grocery store.
They let me stock shelves and wash
lettuce. After about a year,
they paid me a dollar; it was the most
money I had ever made.
I didn't work for the money.
It was just something I enjoyed."*
Bill Raymond

"If a job doesn't keep you awake,
if there's no passion,
then it's not right for you."
Steve Jenkins

"Money is unimportant.
Don't do something just because you
think it will make you rich.
You need to be driven by passion and
excitement, not just money."
Leroy Spears

*"Doing what you love is often your
best chance at wealth."*
Millionaire — net worth 5.9 million

*"True financial independence isn't
having enough money that you never
have to work again; it is having
enough money so that you can be
flexible and do the things
you find most meaningful."*
Millionaire — net worth 2.7 million

Education

"*Many Harvard MBA grads
work for high school grads.
The reason is that
while the first guy was being educated
about the marketplace
the second was experiencing it.*"

Millionaire — net worth 32 million

*"In addition to learning,
education puts you in touch with so
many different people and situations."*
Denny Brown

*"A high school dropout who has
averaged $50,000 a year for ten years
has earned $500,000 by the time a
Doctor graduates from medical school
with $200,000 dollars of debt."*
Millionaire — net worth 6.3 million

Frugality

"When your money is invested,
you can't be taxed.
Invest in tax-free municipals, stocks,
and unrealized gains."
Millionaire — net worth 6 million

"Only the wealthy know exactly how
much they spend on everything."
Millionaire — net worth 36 million

*"You must develop a conservative
attitude in your company —
not only do you have to save money
but teach your employees
to do likewise."*
Millionaire

*"Constantly save, save, save so that
you can capitalize on opportunities —
don't be afraid to take a risk."*
S. Lee Ross

*"People who are self employed
spend more time planning their
financial future.
The company books are their books."*
Millionaire — net worth 5.7 million

*"The people who make the money
are tight, those who inherit it
are spendthrifts."*
Millionaire — net worth 3 million

*"Your annual salary after taxes
should be half of your mortgage,
no less."*
Millionaire — net worth 3.4 million

*"We lived like students even
after I had a job."*
John Simcox

*"The ability to spend
does not determine success."*
Blaine Bowman

*"Don't allow a high income to dictate
an expensive budget."*
Millionaire — net worth 6.2 million

*"There are three kinds of people in this
world: those who live rich,
those who are rich,
and those who live as rich as they are.
The last group is usually
too small to mention."*
Millionaire — net worth 13 million

*"Most of us have found out how to pay
a lower percentage tax rate
than the average American."*
Millionaire — net worth 4.6 million

*"The goal of becoming financially
independent is possible to attain,
but a goal of living the good life
on the way up usually isn't."*
Millionaire — net worth 3.5 million

"No man is rich whose expenditures exceeds his means; and no one is poor whose incomings exceed his outgoings."
Haliburton

"Stocks traded in a pension plan have no capitol gains tax."
Millionaire — net worth 5.4 million

*"Nevada has no state tax,
why else would we live here?"*
Millionaire — net worth 40 million

*"People who live
from paycheck to paycheck
sacrifice wealth for pleasure."*
Millionaire — net worth 3.5 million

*"Wealth is acquired
by focusing on building
an unrealized, non-taxable income."*
Millionaire — net worth 75 million

*"Your net worth should be at least
double your salary."*
Millionaire — net worth 1.5 million

*"Don't buy expensive luggage,
it's too hard for thieves to resist."*
Millionaire — net worth 5 million

*"Know exactly how much you spend on
food, clothing, and housing."*
Millionaire — net worth 3 million

*"One word to describe a future
millionaire — Tightwad."*
Millionaire — net worth 4.3 million

*"Your lifestyle should represent what
you are worth, not what you think you
are going to be worth."*
Millionaire — net worth 3 million

*"I still only order water at
restaurants. I don't need to, but it's
those kind of habits that have helped
me accumulate wealth."*
Millionaire — net worth 200 million

*"What is more important,
living comfortably
with the threat of financial distress
or doing without comfort
once in a while
and having financial security
and peace of mind?"*
Millionaire — net worth 3.5 million

*"Don't support your kids financially
when they leave home."*
Millionaire — net worth 5 million

"When starting your own business,
prepare yourself for the lean years.
Don't think it will
just be lean months."
Millionaire — net worth 5.8 million

"Invest your profits into your own
business, not in the stocks of others."
Millionaire — net worth 2.8 million

"Live within your means —
an attorney can make
$500,000 a year and
still live paycheck to paycheck."
Norm Nemro

"The main principle in my household
is frugal, frugal, frugal —
so I can save
at least 20% of my income."
Charles A. Coonradt

*"The only alternative budgeting is
investing 15% first
and then living on the rest."*
Millionaire — net worth 2 million

*"When starting my new business
I was out of money and resources,
I found out that Lands End would
take anything back for a full refund.
I sent back every article
of clothing I had."*
Millionaire — net worth 30 million

Negotiations

*"I wish I could sell myself for what
people think I'm worth and buy myself
back for what I really am worth."*
Gene Friedman

*"Save every memo and statement so
you can hold people to what they say."*
Millionaire — net worth 1.4 million

"If ever I am in a deal
and the other guy says,
'You can trust me,
I'm a this or that,'
I immediately stand up
and walk away."
Millionaire — net worth 42 million

"Realize that there are pivotal
moments when you should resist
breaking the awkward silence
in a negotiation."
Millionaire — net worth 6.2 million

*"While negotiating, encourage the
other guy to talk up your company,
then you can up the terms of the deal."*
Millionaire — net worth 3.8 million

*"Secret of bartering:
the ability to give an offensive price
without being offensive.
Leave and then give them
a way to contact you."*
Millionaire — net worth 4.8 million

*"Don't imply something in a sale
and then deny it later."*
Millionaire — net worth 5 million

"Be candid where others are deceptive."
Millionaire — net worth 4.6 million

*"Don't try to push a client over
their budget limit."*
Millionaire — net worth 5.6 million

*"Stock in a company is often more
valuable than a high salary."*
Millionaire — net worth 12 million

*"After you've milked someone dry
in a deal, or you think you have,
give a little bit back.
That little bit is worth more to you
as a contribution."*
Millionaire — net worth 30 million

*"Peer pressure is powerful,
even if the customer doesn't know
all of the 'others' who
are demanding your product."*
Millionaire — net worth 3 million

*"When negotiating,
you must first flush out the real
decision maker of the group."*
Millionaire — net worth 4 million

"Don't prolong uncomfortable
parts of a negotiation.
Speak your mind and move on."
Millionaire — net worth 4.8 million

"Find something to agree on
early on in a negotiation."
Millionaire — net worth 5 million

"Never oversell that which you can't
deliver, it always ends ugly."
Millionaire — net worth 2.5 million

"When asking for a raise,
remember to ask for what
you really want
not for what you think you'll get."
Millionaire — net worth 3.8 million

"After you are sold on something,
force yourself to step back
and look at the downside."
Millionaire — net worth 5 million

*"Häagen Dazs has always
been made in New Jersey.
Know what appeals to people,
even in a name."*
Millionaire — net worth 5.8 million

*"Before you negotiate
leave a third person behind
so if you need to,
you can postpone signing
until you 'okay it
with that third person.' "*
Millionaire — net worth 5.6 million

*"If you can't walk away at any time
then you shouldn't be negotiating."*
Steve Jenkins

*"The deal is no good unless everyone
gets a piece of the pie."*
Mel Marion

*"All government—indeed, every
human benefit and every prudent act is
founded on compromise and barter."*
Edmund Burke

*"Always negotiate in private.
Never use publicity to affect the deal."*
Millionaire — net worth 12 million

*"If you want 100,000 units,
ask the price of one million,
then two million —
then you will know the real cost."*
Jonathan Coon

"Sales: find out what the customer
wants and give it to him.
Negotiating: find out what the other
person wants and give it to him.
Success: know what people want and
how to give it to them."
Millionaire — net worth 31 million

"Ideal negotiating: getting to the point
where you both think you're ripping
the other guy off."
Steve Jenkins

"When I was selling my company
I was offered four times what it was
worth. Instead of taking the first offer,
I replied, "You can't be serious."
I ended up selling my company for an
amount six times its actual value."

Millionaire — net worth 65 million

"Never accept the first offer, even if it is
more than you think you are worth.
The bidder thinks his offer is low."

Millionaire — net worth 68 million

"If you want a deal to go through,
start some sort of commerce
with the other party, on the side,
to push it along."
Millionaire — net worth 35 million

"In negotiating,
he who makes the first offer loses."
Millionaire — net worth 6.9 million

"Avoid trouncing your boss or clients in an athletic contest. They will be too depressed by their performance to be impressed by yours."
Millionaire — net worth 1.5 million

"Assume people will be judgmental and will find any concept hard to understand."
Millionaire — net worth 7 million

Proverbs

"Work is the elixir of life."
Kent Archibald

*"He who surpasses or subdues
mankind must look down on the
hate of those below."*
Lord Byron — Millionaire

*"Adversity introduces
a man to himself."*
Anonymous

*"If you torture data long enough,
they will confess."*
MIT T-shirt

"A lottery is a tax on imbeciles."
Italian Expression

*"Behind an able man there
are always other able men."*
Chinese Proverb

*"It's what we learn after we think we
know everything that counts."*
John Wooden

*"The secret to life is to be a day early
and a dollar long —
this way you can own it."*
Charles A. Coonradt

*"False in one thing,
false in everything."*
Charles Sumner

*"He is not only idle who
does nothing, but he is idle
who might be better employed."*
Socrates

*"The first one gets the oyster, the
second gets the shell."*
Andrew Carnegie
— net worth 475 million

*"A wise man knows everything,
a shrewd man knows everyone."*
Millionaire — net worth 29 million

*"For want of a nail the shoe was lost;
for want of a shoe the horse was lost;
and for want of a horse the rider was
lost; being overtaken and slain by the
enemy, all for want of care about a
horseshoe nail."*
**Benjamin Franklin
— net worth $150,000**

*"Always make an audience
suffer as much as possible."*
Alfred Hitchcock

"For advice, seek experience."
Millionaire — net worth 3.5 million

"In fair weather, prepare for foul."
Thomas Fuller

"Those in the free seats hiss first."
Chinese Proverb

"Success covers many blunders."
George Bernard Shaw

*"The circumstances of others
seem good to us
while ours seem good to others."*
Publius Syrus

"If you always live with those who are lame, you yourself will begin to limp."
Latin Proverb

"The best carpenters make the fewest chips."
German Proverb

"Money is the root of all good."
Ayn Rand

*"Have more than thou showest,
speak less than thou knowest."*
Shakespeare

*"Never answer a letter
while you are angry."*
Chinese Proverb

*"Give me the ready hand
rather than the ready tongue."*
Giuseppe Garibaldi

*"Doubt the man who
swears to his devotion."*
Mme. Louise Colet

*"Think before you leap,
but don't think too long."*
Millionaire — net worth 6 million

*"Eighty percent of success
is showing up."*
Woody Allen

*"The secret to business is to know
something that nobody else knows."*
Aristotle Onassis

*"Even the lion has to defend himself
against the flies."*
— German Proverb

"Plough deep while sluggards sleep."
Benjamin Franklin
— net worth $150,000

*"If you help people get what they want,
they will help you get what you want."*
Hal Wing

*A competitor is the guy who goes
in a revolving door behind you
and comes out ahead of you."*
George Romney

*"A short pencil
is better than a long memory."*
Ben Franklin
— net worth $150,000

*"Bring order into your kingdom and
your kingdom will expand."*
Larry Bair

*"If you've got time to lean
you've got time to clean."*
Keath Bills

"Persistence is omnipotent."
Jonathan Coon

Family

"Put your family first."
Millionaire — net worth 152 million

"Your home is your second business;
operate it like one."
Millionaire — net worth 25 million

"If your wife spends lavishly,
you won't make it for long
no matter what your income is."
Millionaire — net worth 4 million

"Without my wife's keen advice,
I would be a poor man."
J. D. Rockefeller 1839-1937
— net worth 1.4 billion

*"Use a role model to show employees
where they will be someday
if they work hard."*
Millionaire — net worth 25 million

*"Choose a nonpartisan third party
to be the executor of your will.
It is better for your children
to be mad at the guy in the middle
than at each other."*
Millionaire — net worth 32 million

*"Never hire friends or family; it's not
just for the reasons you think."*
Millionaire — net worth 17 million

*"Teach your children
to be over-achievers
not over-achiever consumers."*
Millionaire — net worth 3.4 million

*"Does your mother say she loves you?
Check it out."*
Chicago Newspaper Maxim

"I cheat my boys every chance I get.
I want to make 'em sharp."
John D. Rockefeller
— net worth 1.4 billion

"Leave your children enough money
so they can do anything
but not do nothing."
Warren Buffett
— net worth 12 billion

"Teach your children to be frugal
no matter how rich you are."
Millionaire — net worth 3.5 million

"*Don't bring your problems at work
home to your family.*"
Millionaire — net worth 17 million

"*Never control your children
with your money.*"
Millionaire — net worth 15 million

"*Tell your children of your true wealth
only after they have proven themselves
self-sufficient.*"
Millionaire — net worth 15 million

*"Don't bring friends or family into
your business and don't borrow money
from the wrong people."*
Hal Wing

*"Estate Planning—
start a business for your kids
and then make it valuable.
Then you don't have to worry
about Uncle Sam taking
half before your kids get it."*
Paul Hulme

Employees

*"Loyalty: if your employees think
they're still expendable
after 20 years,
how could they be loyal to you?"*
Millionaire — net worth 5 million

*"When selecting employees I value
enthusiasm, integrity, and analytical
ability more than experience."*
Blaine Bowman

*"Employees, like soldiers, need to know
they will be rewarded for success and
court-marshaled if they don't try."*
Millionaire — net worth 15 million

*"The only thing worse than all bad
news is all good news, [which usually
means] someone isn't telling you
about their screw-ups."*
Millionaire — net worth 25 million

*"Only confront people when you have
absolute proof—you don't want
to be caught flat-footed."*
Millionaire — net worth 5.7 million

*"Excellence and superior performance
must be pursued and rewarded.
We held annual performance reviews
where employees evaluated
their own performance
as well as that of their supervisors."*
Kyle Bowen Love

*"I've always let my managers run
things like they own them."*
Millionaire — net worth 24 million

*"Motivate people with the feeling
of being a part of something
unique and great."*
Millionaire — net worth 5 million

*"Compliment people behind their
back; they always find out."*
Millionaire — net worth 2 million

*"Don't settle for someone
who is a hard worker
but has bad judgement."*
Millionaire — net worth 4.1 million

*"If someone makes a part wrong
I go directly to the person,
not the foreman."*
Hal Wing

*"Don't wait to perform
at the level of your superiors."*
Millionaire — net worth 6.5 million

*"For more information,
get people away from the office
[and] into a social setting."*
Millionaire — net worth 3.4 million

*"Don't ever tell people the truth
about themselves
when it's negative
and can't be rectified."*
Millionaire — net worth 3.2 million

"*When someone is wrong
make it as easy as possible
for them to correct their mistake.*"
Millionaire — net worth 9.5 million

"*People are unproductive and waste
time because they have no reward for
finishing tasks, just one for lasting
until the end of the day.*"
Millionaire — net worth 3 million

*"Big companies often humble their new
employees with heavy workloads,
forcing them to become team players
while simultaneously weeding out
the faint of heart."*
Millionaire — net worth 6 million

*"Don't treat receptionists like they
don't affect you because they can."*
Millionaire — net worth 27 million

*"The best way to get all of the
information out of a subordinate
is by not getting angry
before they have confessed
everything they know."*
Millionaire — net worth 5 million

*"Never tell anyone how to do
something, just tell them
what needs to be done — let them
surprise you with their ingenuity."*
— Patton

*"A waiter can make the
difference between you getting
the best seat in the house
or the one by the bathroom door.
Everyone has influence
in their respective realm."*
Millionaire — net worth 13 million

*"People seldom improve
when they have no other model but
themselves to copy after."*
Goldsmith

"Never reprimand anyone in public."
Millionaire — net worth 2.9 million

"Spend your time working with
your best employees,
not coddling your worst ones."
Millionaire — net worth 6.2 million

"Everyone in your company
must have a measurable goal
with a deadline."
Millionaire — net worth 4.9 million

"Giving credit where credit is due
always comes back as credit to you."
Millionaire — net worth 4 million

"Don't confront employees with their
mistakes when they are down;
wait until they get overconfident
about their performance
and too big for their britches."
Millionaire — net worth 3 million

"You must provide a way for people to
know if they are winning or losing
on a daily basis."
Charles A. Coonradt

"When hiring, look for a continued pattern of success."
Blaine Bowman

*"Don't talk about your net worth to your employees.
Don't talk about it to your mother."*
Millionaire — net worth 10 million

"You gotta make enough to hire smart people so they can make it for you."
Bill Brady

"We hire individuals for their imagination and creativity as much as we do for their education and experience."

John Walton

"The best way to motivate people is to make them feel important."

Millionaire — net worth 6.3 million

*"Only intuition can protect you from
hiring the most dangerous individual
of all, the articulate incompetent."*
**Robert Bernstein,
President of Random House**

*"The CEO of Intel has a cubicle
the same size as his employees."*
Millionaire — net worth 21 million

*"The secret of Attila the Hun
was that he fought ferociously
side by side with his men."*
Millionaire — net worth 6.5 million

*"Your greatest asset
is not your product, machines,
technology, or stock;
it's your people."*
Hal Wing

*"Many people are intelligent,
only a few are committed."*
Eric Jackson

*"We look for people with degrees in
English, History, Psychology, Art, etc.
and teach them about business.
If they have a varied background
and a curious mind
we can teach them how to be successful
in business in a few months."*
John Walton

*"Choose employees who are
strong where you are weak."*
Millionaire — net worth 2.9 million

*"Treat your employees
like your best customer.
We provided profit sharing
and stock options.
We held monthly staff meetings
where we openly discussed the
status of the company,
handed out profit sharing checks,
and received feedback from employees.
We gave them a frank assessment of
the state of the company.
Every job in the company
is essential and important."*

Kyle Bowen Love

*"Enthusiasm is infectious.
People can't resist even when they
know what you are trying to do."*
Millionaire — net worth 36 million

*"Work hard to give your employees a
sense of ownership."*
Millionaire — net worth 3.9 million

*"Michael Jordan alone could never
beat the worst team in the NBA.."*
Millionaire — net worth 6 million

*"I believe the most significant factor
in the success of our different business
ventures is the quality and
independence of our workers
from the top to the bottom."*
John Walton

*"I made the first five-hundred-
thousand and then others helped me
make the last twenty million.
My greatest talent was the ability to
surround myself with good people."*
Bill Brady

Isn't it the truth

*"Big spenders may get all of the
publicity, but they aren't a good
representation of the wealthy."*
Millionaire — net worth 5 million

*"Offense gets the glory,
but defense wins the game."*
Millionaire — net worth 2.3 million

*"It is double pleasure
to deceive the deceiver."*
La Fontaine

*"Never divulge anything
self-incriminating to
a friendly associate."*
Millionaire — net worth 5 million

*"Learn to not spin
your wheels in meetings."*
Millionaire — net worth 5 million

*"As a salesman you should
ask everyone to buy."*
Millionaire — net worth 5.2 million

*"If the sales pitch is long, it means the
product needs a lot of building up to be
appealing or the price is too high."*
Millionaire — net worth 12 million

*"Who you are in ten years
depends on who you associate with
between now and then."*
Millionaire — net worth 7.5 million

*"Avoid network marketing unless
you're the one starting the company."*
Millionaire — net worth 3.4 million

*"It's a good idea to have a stable job
and test entrepreneurial ideas
on the side."*
Millionaire — net worth 5.3 million

*"Millionaires tend to exercise;
habits of productivity transfer
to all areas of life."*
Millionaire — 200 million

*"Almost every good idea has been
rejected at least once.
Every bad idea has too."*
Millionaire — net worth 3.7 million

*"Sales is not just a numbers game
until you have perfected every other
aspect of your presentation."*
Millionaire — net worth 5.4 million

*"You'll never win a sale
by winning a debate."*
Millionaire — net worth 5.4 million

*"Favors poorly executed
are worse than none at all."*
Millionaire — net worth 3 million

*"It's easier to buy rich clothes than to
actually have money."*
Millionaire — net worth 1.5 million

"Be leery of people who try to solicit
anything on the phone.
If you want the best
you usually have to go out
and find it."
Millionaire — net worth 53 million

"Wall Street is the only place where
people ride in a Rolls Royce
to get advice from people
who take the subway."
Warren Buffet
— net worth 12 billion

"Beware of a client or company that is,
'All hat and no cattle.' "
Millionaire — net worth 2.5 million

"The more you say, the less people
remember. The fewer the words,
the greater the prophet."
Fénelon

"I was an instant success
due to years of hard work."
Millionaire — net worth 35 million

*"Good advertising isn't based
on just how many people see it,
but also on how many people
it convinces."*
Millionaire — net worth 5 million

*"The last people to come to your aid
will be the bankers."*
Millionaire — net worth 62 million

"Memos: the shorter the better."
Millionaire — net worth 4 million

"*Learning from your mistakes is good,
learning from other's mistakes is just
as good and usually cheaper.*"
Steve Jenkins

"*Never tell your secrets to the media,
but receive them with hospitality.*"
Millionaire — net worth 6 million

"*Most smokers end up spending more
on cigarettes than their home.*"
Millionaire — net worth 13 million

*"When you talk to important people
write down what you talked about.
They will be impressed when you
remember it the next time you meet."*
Millionaire — net worth 6 million

*"Some good ideas never make money
while other bad ideas make millions.
Success often depends
on people's perception."*
Millionaire — net worth 3 million

*"One thing people don't realize is that
when they confront the boss,
no matter how right they are,
they can still get fired."*
Millionaire — net worth 23 million

*"If people treat you like royalty
because you are a CEO,
you can be sure they would expect
the same treatment."*
Millionaire — net worth 5.2 million

"Round numbers are always false."
Samuel Johnson

*"Even the President can't plan his day
and be sure it won't be interrupted."*
Millionaire — net worth 4.8 million

*"Be quick to capitalize on opportunity
but don't make a show of it."*
Millionaire — net worth 3.2 million

*"A business plan is to convince your
banker not just your mother.
Be realistic."*
Millionaire — net worth 2.4 million

*"It's usually the owners and their top
salesman who have more leeway in
negotiating the price."*
Millionaire — net worth 3.9 million

*"When you make plans too far in
advance, you end up losing even more
time trying to break them later."*
Millionaire — net worth 2.5 million

"Time is the only resource we own,
money isn't."
Steve Jenkins

"Remember that your failure
is another man's opportunity."
Millionaire — net worth 4 million

When you apologize,
don't make too big of a deal out of it.
As Holmes says, "Apology is only
egoism wrong side out."
Millionaire — net worth 5.3 million

*"Don't be distracted by success
and its enticements —
focus and discipline
bring continued results."*
John Simcox

*"Winners are motivated
to do better by disappointment
while losers use it
as an excuse to quit."*
Millionaire — net worth 3.6 million

" 'Sink or swim' is often
the best motivation."
Millionaire — net worth 54 million

"When people say,
'It ain't the money it's the principle,'
you can be sure it's the money."
Millionaire — net worth 4.8 million

"Just because you're paranoid doesn't
mean they're not out to get you."
Blaine Bowman

"Reality is never the extreme —
neither your greatest hopes
nor greatest fears are ever realized.
Reality is in the middle."
John E. Ord

"When business is good,
it pays to advertise.
When business is bad,
you have to advertise."
Millionaire — net worth 26 million

*"Thinking is the hardest work
there is."*
Henry Ford — net worth 1.2 billion

*"In business, stealing a man's time is
the same as his money."*
Millionaire — net worth 4.5 million

*"Two minutes of inspiration
can be more valuable
than 20 years of perspiration."*
Millionaire — net worth 10 million

"You've got to be successful tomorrow.
You can't rest on yesterday."
Mel Marion

"There is usually a difference
between what the critics want
and what the people want."
Millionaire — net worth 5.6 million

"Business plans aren't accurate
models for your business, they are
sales pitches to your investors."
Millionaire — net worth 3.4 million

*"If you always have a pillow to land on
when you fail or quit,
it's hard to ever be desperate enough
to do what it takes."*
Millionaire — net worth 2.7 million

"Beware the fury of a patient man."
John Dryden

*"The richest man in the world is
famous but most of the world's
millionaires are low profile."*
Millionaire — net worth 170 million

"A workaholic will eventually
be less productive sick
than if he would have taken time off."
Millionaire — net worth 4.5 million

"Salesman leave great first
impressions. The problem is
the second impression
is often the same act."
Millionaire — net worth 5 million

*"Your good ideas will be overrated by
you and underrated by others."*
Millionaire — net worth 3.9 million

*"Don't wear a Timex to a meeting
with Casio."*
Millionaire — net worth 2.8 million

*"Success depends more on attention to
detail than good ideas."*
Millionaire — net worth 6.5 million

"I had just started my business and my girlfriend dumped me because I was working too many hours without results. I was watching TV and I'll never forget what Kaptain Kangaroo said to Mr. Greenjeans — 'The best that I can is the best that I can and I'm doing the best that I can."

Dan Galorath — Founder of Galorath

"Under pressure, think about what will matter most in five years."
Millionaire — net worth 5 million

"The harder a salesman works, the more obligated people feel to buy."
Millionaire — net worth 6.2 million

"When taking someone's time, think of how much they make per minute and then ask yourself, 'How valuable is your problem?' "
Millionaire — net worth 4.8 million

*"The best ideas are the ones
people respond to with,
'I should have thought of that.'"*
Millionaire — net worth 6.3 million

*"Failure is more frequently from want
of energy than from want of capital."*
Daniel Webster

*"If you're not satisfied with the terms
it's better to express yourself with
words than with shoddy work."*
Millionaire — net worth 5 million

"Some people accomplish more in one
day than others accomplish
in two weeks."
Millionaire — net worth 3 million

"The worst times to talk business
during lunch is at the beginning and
at the end."
Millionaire — net worth 2.3 million

"Success is oftentimes choosing
between comfort and peace of mind."
Millionaire — net worth 4.5 million

"*Buy companies that any idiot can run
because someday one will.*"
Warren Buffett
— net worth 12 billion

"*People have a tendency to think
they know everything
after they make a little money.*"
Steve Jenkins

"*First make friends
and then make business.*"
Gene Friedman

*"Always remember not to take
everything people say at face value."*
Millionaire — net worth 5.8 million

*"When an argument starts,
progress has ended."*
Millionaire — net worth 4.9 million

*"The most flattering thing a person
could do for me is ask my opinion
and then follow it."*
Millionaire — net worth 2 million

*"Most creative ideas seem so obvious
after someone makes a million bucks
off of them."*

Millionaire — net worth 5.2 million

*"If you don't want to reach someone,
call them at lunch."*

Millionaire — net worth 6.5 million

Persistence

*"Lincoln ran for city council,
state legislature, and Congress
and lost them all."*
Millionaire — net worth 1.2 million

*"If you knock long enough
and loud enough you will
eventually wake someone up."*
Millionaire — net worth 7 million

"Never let go!
Too many give up too early.
Too many give up not realizing how
close to success they were.
Believe in your dream even if everyone
around you has awaken from theirs.
This game is the pursuit of opportuni-
ties without regard for resources.
Fifty rejections is a good start.
Fifty rejections is not enough.
If you prefer to play rather than be a
spectator, you will succeed.
Success is rarely a solo effort.
There is a positive aspect to everything.
Find it."

John Knab

"Persistence often gets you the best job;
most employers are so busy
that they would rather hire the guy
they keep bumping into
than look through a stack of resumes."
Millionaire — net worth 67 million

"Failure ceases to exist
in the face of persistence."
William D. Price

Biographies
(short snipets about the lives of famous millionaires)

Andrew Carnegie
*When Carnegie was asked by his
assistant Charles M. Schwab
about what to do when he had
just thought of a way to save another
half dollar a ton, but it would mean
tearing down the new mill—
Carnegie replied,
"Go ahead and tear it down."*

*As a young man, Andrew Carnegie
returned $500 dollars he had found.
This was equal to ten years of wages
during his time.*

*Carnegie suggested his epitaph read
"Here lies a man who was able to
surround himself with men
far cleverer than himself."*

Sam Walton

Sam Walton, a billionaire and founder of Wal-Mart, drives an old, beat-up pickup truck and gets his hair cut at a local barbershop.

Bill Gates

In 1980 Bill Gates was asked by IBM to create an operating system for their new personal computer. Microsoft had never written one before so it bought one from another company and modified it for the IBM computer. The system is now known as MS DOS.

John D. Rockefeller
*To cut costs, Rockefeller hired his own
wagons to haul barrels of oil and he
built his own barrels. This cut the cost
from $2.50 to 96 cents per barrel.*

Charles Tiffany
*After the first three days of business
Charles L. Tiffany only made $5.00.*

Cornelius Vanderbilt

*Vanderbilt donated his best steamship
to the Union during the Civil War.*

*Vanderbilt made millions from the
gold rush without ever looking for gold.
He transported people by boat
to California.*

*Vanderbilt was tight.
He would carry cigars separately
instead of in a cigar case, because
didn't want to offer them to others.*

Vanderbilt made his money by under-
cutting his competitors prices, often
times losing his own money, until they
paid him to leave the area.

Henry Ford

When offered a billion dollars for his
company, Henry Ford answered,
"I'd have the money, but no job."

John Dodge

John Dodge tested his cars by
personally running one into a brick
wall at 20 mph.

William Wrigley Jr.
Wrigley made a daring advertising move by sending a sample of his new gum to every person listed in the U. S. phone book.

Warren Buffet
As a teenager Warren Buffet bought old pinball machines for $25 and placed them in barbershops. He took home $50 a week.

By age 16 Warren Buffet had accumulated $6000. The year was 1946.

John Pierpont Morgan

J.P. Morgan's goal was not to
accumulate the largest fortune but to
create an enduring organization.

Johns Hopkins

Johns Hopkins left school at the age
of twelve and yet because
of his fortune and contributions,
his name will always be associated
with higher learning.

Walt Disney

When on the brink of bankruptcy
Walt Disney played the voice of
Mickey Mouse himself.

Lee Iaccoca

Lee Iaccoca decided in college that he
wanted to be a vice president of
Ford Motor Company;
at age 35 he was.

Other titles published by World Leisure

Getting to Know You
by Jeanne McSweeney & Charles Leocha
$6.95

Getting to Know Kids in Your Life
by Jeanne McSweeney & Charles Leocha
$6.95

Travel Rights
by Charles Leocha $9.95

A Woman's ABCs of Life
by Beca Lewis $6.95

Great Adventure Vacations with Your Kids
by Dorothy Jordon $11.95

Great Nature Vacations with Your Kids
by Dorothy Jordon $9.95

*Available in bookstores or
through www.worldleisure.com
and www.amazon.com*